# Desert S

by Layne

## Table of Contents

Consultant:
Adria F. Klein, Ph.D.
California State University, San Bernardino

capstone
classroom
Heinemann Raintree • Red Brick Learning
division of Capstone

# The Sonoran Desert

The Sonoran Desert is in the southwest corner of the United States. It stretches across parts of Arizona and California. It is a place of remarkable beauty.

It is warm here most of the year.
There are still changes in the weather
from season to season, including
storms like this one. There are also
many amazing plants and animals
that live here. The Sonoran Desert
is home to a rich **ecosystem**.

# Spring

Spring comes in late February.
The days are warm. Lizards enjoy
the sunshine. Birds build nests, lay
eggs, and get ready for new babies.

Desert flowers also bloom in spring. Colorful blossoms cover the desert. Wildflowers provide food for insects and butterflies. Spring in the desert usually lasts until the end of April.

# Summer

In the summer, the weather is dry.
The saguaro cactus flowers bloom.
Bats that fly north from Mexico
come to feed on the flowers.

The bats help to **pollinate** the flowers as they fly from one cactus to another. This helps fruit to grow on each cactus. Later, other desert animals will eat the cactus fruit.

May and June are the driest months of the desert summer. July and August are rainy months. They are also the hottest. Huge rainstorms called **monsoons** roll across the desert.

Plants and animals need the water that falls during this rainy season. Toads and other **amphibians** come out to enjoy the damp weather. Prickly pear cactuses and other plants bear fruit. Fruit is an important source of food for birds flying through on their way south.

# Fall

In September, the weather is cooler and dryer. It is fall in the desert. The weather is still warm enough for plants to blossom.

It is cool enough for more animals to come out during the day. In the hot summer, many animals escape the heat and sleep all day. Now they can be out in the sun. Other fall animals include **migrating** birds that stop on their way to warmer climates.

# Winter

Winter begins in December.
The weather is cooler and rainy.
Sometimes it even snows!
Winter is the second wettest time
of the year in the Sonoran Desert.

Mockingbirds, woodpeckers, and wrens are some of the desert's winter visitors. Other animals like hot weather best. Some of them such as lizards and toads **hibernate** underground in the winter.

In February, winter ends and spring
returns once more. Wildflowers
bloom and animals like this tortoise
come out to soak up the sunshine.
The **cycle** of seasons begins again.
The desert blooms once more.

# Glossary

**amphibian**    an animal that is born in the water, then lives most of its adult life on land

**cycle**    events that happen over and over again in the same pattern

**ecosystem**    all the plants and animals that make up an area

**hibernate**    to sleep during the winter

**migrate**    to move from one place to another, often because of changes in the weather

**monsoon**    a storm that brings a lot of rain

**pollinate**    to move pollen from one part of a flower (stamen) to another part (pistil)

# Index